The Owl Book

by Jane Russ

GRAFFEG

Dedication

For my grandsons Arlo and Rudy
Jenkins, in the hope that the natural
world will be as important to them as
it has always been to me.

Contents

Introduction

Owls seem simple, but in reality they are quite complicated.

To begin with, worldwide there are hundreds of different types of owl. They live in all kinds of habitats and come in an enormous range of sizes. Even the answer to a simple question like, 'what is the largest owl?' is disputed, with the great grey owl winning in terms of length but generally considered to be beaten for weight by the Eurasian eagle owl and Blakiston's fish owl.

The question, 'which owls are native to the United Kingdom?' has a flexible answer too. The barn, tawny, short-eared and long-eared owls are the four true natives. The little owl, although quite common, is actually a continental addition. The snowy owl has been found within these islands (actually only one, Fetlar in the Shetlands) classed as a 'rare visitor'. Finally, the eagle owl has small pockets of escapees breeding successfully and there are questions being asked about a native status for them as well.

Owls have a complicated, almost contradictory, relationship with man too. On the one hand available in all purchasable formats; as sculptures, mugs, cushions, bags, hats, they are knitted on jumpers, crocheted on throws, and taken into our homes as loved and revered characters. Perceived as wise, learned and heavily anthropomorphised by children and adults alike, their upright stance, large eyes and beak 'nose' making us feel they are knowing and lovable. On the other hand, they are killing machines of the

Left: Barn Owl

most perfect kind, with outstanding hearing, almost silent flight when hunting, and talons and a beak with which to despatch prey with the accuracy of a scalpel.

In many cultures they are feared as harbingers of death, their ethereal call in the night sending shivers through a household. More often heard rather than seen much about their nocturnal life remains mysterious. One can imagine only too easily how, in a less scientific age, where the source of the hooting/screeching/hissing and moaning was unknown, stories would flourish of the 'spirit in the night'. The almost silent flight of a white barn owl through evening mist could very easily be a will-o'-the-wisp.

Conversely, they were also considered the farmer's friend, keeping down vermin in and around the farm. In Roman times their breeding needs were incorporated into the design of barns and grain stores, owl access being an automatic design feature of any large farm structure. Only modern barns made of steel and concrete have omitted these, thus necessitating the construction of nest boxes by conservationists, with varying degrees of success.

Currently the consensus is that there are 216 species of owl in the world divided into two families: 18 *Tytonidae* – the barn owl family, and 198 *Strigidae* – the typical owl family. All owls are of the order *Strigiformes* but you can understand that, to ensure which specific owl we are talking about, it is necessary to work down through its antecedents naming family, genus, Latin name and common name.

Owls found in the UK

Family	Genus	Latin name	Common name
Tytonidae	*Tyto*	*tyto alba*	barn owl
Strigidae	*Strix*	*strix aluco*	tawny owl
Strigidae	*Asio*	*asio flammeus*	short-eared owl
Strigidae	*Asio*	*asio otus*	long-eared owl
Strigidae	*Athene*	*athene noctua*	little owl
Strigidae	*Bubo (nyctea)*	*bubo scandiaca (nyctea scandiaca)*	snowy owl
Strigidae	*Bubo*	*bubo bubo*	eagle owl

barn owl   tawny owl   short-eared owl   long-eared owl   little owl   snowy owl   eagle owl

How the owl turns its head and other interesting physical facts

Even an owl cannot turn its head in a full circle, that is just a myth.

However, the crucial issue is that owls don't have eyeballs like humans, their eye is more like a tube. Consequently they can't move their eyes in their sockets, they have to move their whole head. The owl can turn its head up to 270 degrees to left or right from the front facing position. Under normal circumstances, if they had the system of a human and did this, they would die from a stroke because of the loss of blood flow to the brain. However, as discovered by a team at Johns Hopkins University School of Medicine in the USA, led by medical illustrator Fabian de Kok-Mercado, there are several reasons why this doesn't happen.

To start with, an owl has twice as many vertebrae in its neck as a human; fourteen in total. Arteries to the brain travel up the neck through the vertebrae and from there into the head. Furthermore, twelve of the fourteen owl vertebrae have a larger cavity at their core than normal, up to ten times the diameter of the artery travelling through it. The extra space contains an air sac which gives the artery a support cushion to allow for movement inside the neck when the head is turned.

The study at John Hopkins began with twelve dead owls, (snowy, barred and great horned owls) after their deaths from natural causes. The creation of 3D images of the bones and related blood vessels is thought to be the first time angiography, CT scans and medical illustration have been used in this way. An associate professor in the Russell H. Morgan Department of Radiology at Johns Hopkins, Philippe Gailloud, has said that he had wondered why rapid, twisting head movements did not leave thousands of owls lying dead on the forest floor from stroke. "The carotid and vertebral arteries in the neck of most animals – including owls and humans – are very fragile and highly susceptible to even minor tears of the vessel lining." Contrast dye was used in the dead owls to make the clearest X-ray images possible and this, combined with painstaking dissection, led to highly detailed analysis of the data.

The research team under Kok-Mercado and Gailloud noticed that as dye was added to the blood vessels at the base of the head, just under the jaw, the blood vessels kept expanding and the fluid pooled in reservoirs unlike in human anatomy

where the tendency is to contract. The researchers understood that this pooling enabled the owls brain and eyes to continue functioning without disruption during any rotation of the head. The owls were also found to have many interconnections and free adaptations in their vascular network, which meant they could bypass the usual routes for blood when a turn is initiated but keep the blood flowing. Furthermore, the vertebral artery goes into an owl's

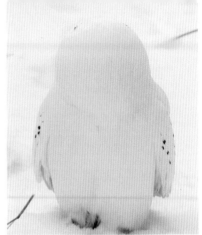

neck higher up than in other birds allowing for more slack in the artery. Owls are not the only birds who can turn their heads in this way but the extra space in the vertebrae for the artery is unique.

Surprisingly, owls have three eyelids. The top eyelid closes down and is for blinking, the bottom eyelid closes upwards and is for sleeping. Perhaps the most interesting is the third clear or slightly opaque eyelid called the nictitating membrane. This moves from the inside corner of the eye, nearest the beak, to the outside edge of the eye, covering the whole eye and closing horizontally. With this eyelid, owls have extra protection for these very sensitive and vital organs but they can still see when they are closed. It can be imagined that flying with eyes open can dry the surface and the membrane not only protects the eyeball but allows it to stay moisturised.

Another unusual physical and very specialised attribute of owls, is that they have zygodactyl toes with an extra swivel joint.

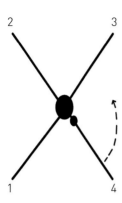

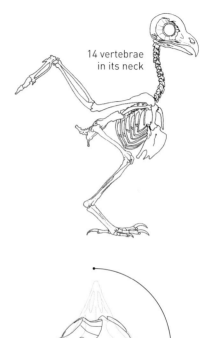

14 vertebrae
in its neck

They have four toes, with 2, 3 and 4 usually facing forwards, particularly in flight or when sitting on a flat surface, and number 1 facing backwards. However, when catching prey or needing a solid roosting position, they can swivel the outer toe (4) to the back to provide a two and two format for an extra fearsome grip. This flexible joint is unusual and only found in some other birds of prey.

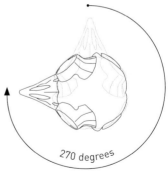

270 degrees

The owl can turn its head up to 270 degrees to left or right from the front facing position.

Barn Owl

Barn Owl

Family *tytonidae*
Genus *tyto*
Latin Name *tyto alba*
Common Name barn owl
Length 29–44cm
Wing span approx 85–95cm
Females generally 5–10% longer than males
Weight 240–425g
Females generally 20–40% heavier than males

Found on every continent except Antarctica, the barn owl is the most widespread land bird species in the world, falling mainly between 40°N and 40°S of the equator. It was first described in 1769 by the physician and naturalist Giovanni Antonio Scopoli in his *Anni Historico-Naturales*. In the British Isles the barn owl has a warm goldy apricot coloured back and head, with fine delicate flecking of grey and narrow black and white patterning on individual feathers. The breast, facial disk and legs are white, with a heart-shaped frame edging the disk and, with the dark eyes and beak, it has an almost human look; the beak standing in for the nose. The legs, unlike some other species, have very close feathering in white, with almost bare claws, with talons, unlike other raptors, having two toes forward and two toes back.

In the past, Britain's most common owl species was the barn owl. Today however, numbers have dropped considerably and it has been estimated that only one farm in seventy five has a nesting owl. The perfect barn owl habitat is farmland/grassland/rough grazing, with

wide field margins, light woodland, hedgerows, where a daytime roost might be in a hollow tree or outbuildings.

The most important thing about any habitat is that there must be high numbers of rodents, short-tailed field voles are a special favourite, along with mice and common shrews. They will also take small birds, together with the occasional frog. It has been estimated that a breeding pair need to find and catch upwards of 5,000 meals a year and it is easy to understand that if there is a bulge in the small mammal population, barn owl numbers will grow. Similarly, they are very susceptible to a sudden drop in the amount of food stock available and numbers may fall to dangerous levels in, for instance, a year with a very wet spring.

When hunting, the barn owl uses sound more than sight. The heart-shaped facial disk draws in sounds, rather as a human ear does, giving the barn owl very acute hearing. The ears are set with one higher than the other, just inside the edge of the heart shape, next to the eyes. This asymmetry of the ears means that sound information is coming from more than one plane, meaning it can hunt in total darkness with amazing accuracy, almost as if guided by radar.

Prey is found by quartering the ground, back and forth at a height of between two to five metres. They use a virtually silent flap and glide technique, which they have because their flight feathers are softly fringed rather than crisply fringed, resulting in no 'snap in the flap'. Sometimes a fence post or low tree branch will

be used as a vantage point to listen for that tell-tale rustle through the vegetation.

The undulating swooping glide is often topped with a swirling turn and stoop before the plunge into the undergrowth to seize the prey.

The barn owl, like most owls is nocturnal, most often seen at, or just before, dusk. They do sometimes hunt during daylight hours but this usually depends on whether there are other birds around to mob them. Gulls, rooks and magpies are the keenest to mob, as are small birds, having a lifelong anxiety about owls; they are, after all, an additional food source for many, particularly long-eared owls in the winter. Although normally very wary of owls when alone, if an old or injured owl is roosting quietly in the daytime, small birds like finches, tits and buntings may begin to mob it. This mobbing starts with the birds gathering and calling loudly to one another, with a display of wings slightly open and legs bent. A 'crowd mentality' gradually takes over and new small birds turning up late to the event, will join in the shouting and gang display, without even really seeing the owl. Larger birds like blackbirds may even risk dive-bombing the owl. Eventually the besieged owl, who by this time tends to be rather irritated by the whole thing, will flap off and find a quieter place to sit. The calling and general racket may go on for some time after the owl has left, the small birds taking a while to calm down.

Single birds will mob too, as in the picture on the left, taken on the Somerset Levels in which a kestrel is after an easy meal, trying to steal the prey of the barn owl.

It is possible that diurnal hunting is the result of insufficient catches the night before, usually caused by poor weather conditions. Under severe conditions owls will starve, being unable to find sufficient prey.

Catches are generally swallowed whole or pulled to shreds if there are young to feed. As with all raptors, barn owls disgorge undigested food in pellets. These are usually comprised of bones, fur, and if small birds have been taken, feathers. Pellets can be found around nests or regular roosting sites and are an intense and shiny black. Analysis of these pellets will show exactly what the owls are feeding on.

Nests are not always built in agricultural buildings. Caves and tree hollows are an alternative, as well as specially constructed nest boxes used to encourage breeding where numbers have fallen. Breeding takes place from around March or April, depending on the weather. The number of eggs (or even whether breeding takes place at all) is very much linked to the availability of food. In a lean year there might only be three or four of the oval, white eggs in one clutch but in a good year, with plenty of food and good weather conditions, that number could rise to seven or eight and there might be two clutches during the season. Over the last thirty years, barn owl numbers have fallen dramatically, so much so that the barn owl is protected under Schedule 1 of the Wildlife and Countryside Act (1981) and anyone found intentionally

The owlets, which are originally covered in soft white down, will be fledged and disperse at two to three months.

disturbing the birds during the breeding process can be prosecuted.

Barn owl nests are not filled with the usual nesting materials seen in those of other birds. In fact generally the eggs will be nestled into a bed of pellets. It takes just over a month to incubate the eggs and whilst the majority of this is done by the female, the male will be in attendance, feeding her and the chicks as they hatch. Obviously a new mate would be found if one were killed but generally speaking, barn owls do mate for life. Interestingly, because the eggs are laid at two day intervals, the chicks hatch gradually so in a clutch of four eggs, the last to hatch might be in the nest with a fully feathered youngster from the same brood. Furthermore, in some

broods, rare bird behaviour has been recorded, where the chicks will feed each other.

The owlets, which are originally covered in soft white down, will be fledged and disperse at two to three months but the majority will not survive their first year, a substantial number of juveniles being killed on motorways or beside busy roads. Grass verges are the perfect surroundings for small rodents that make up the main diet of the barn owl but that comes with the added danger of fast cars. In the wild a barn owl will, on average, live between one and five years. In captivity or in a safer environment, they can live up to twenty years.

A high percentage of barn owls examined when dead had rat poison in their systems. Naturally, this would kill some but others had non-lethal doses. However, it isn't yet known what effect these lower doses have on those it doesn't kill.

The barn owl does not hoot, that is the tawny owl or other members of the genus *strix*. Instead, the barn owl is the perpetrator of that eerie shriek you hear in the night, most often rather drawn out and chilling. It has been suggested that the shriek, combined with silent flight and sudden appearance of an owl can frighten its prey to death. When courting, males 'twitter' and a hiss like bottled gas escaping is used by young and old alike to ward off intruders. Barn owls have two strategies if cornered and frightened; one is that they throw themselves onto their backs and use those razor sharp talons as a defence and the other is that they will play dead.

Tawny Owl

Tawny Owl

Family *strigidae*
Genus *strix*
Latin Name *strix aluco*
Common Name tawny owl
Length 36–46cm
Wing span approx 85–105cm
Females generally 5–10% longer than males
Weight 330–700g
Females generally 20–40% heavier than males

The tawny owl is the commonest and most familiar owl over most of Europe. However, an accurate total for the number of breeding pairs in the UK is very hard to come by; being nocturnal and very well camouflaged in their daytime roosts. The best guesstimate as of mid-2017 is between 15,000 and 40,000 pairs. There are more breeding tawnies than any other owl species in the UK and they are found in numbers in England, Scotland and Wales. Recently, for the first time, tawny owls have been found breeding in the east of Ireland. Traditionally, it was thought they would not fly over water but this Ireland cohort, together with a colony on the Isle of Man seems to dispute this theory.

In 2010 the British Trust for Ornithology undertook a survey which revealed that numbers were stable. Two studies between 1990 and 2003 have concluded that tawny owls, unlike other owls in the UK, were not affected by a rise in the use of pesticides in previous years. Farming methods have caused some decline in numbers as natural nesting sites (tawnies are particularly keen on reusing nests) in hollow trees and mixed woodland

have been lost due to over-coppicing and building. On the plus side, more nest boxes are being provided as people begin to understand the importance of conservation.

The tawny owl has a round head and a solid stocky body, the archetypal 'owl shape' we know from children's story books, and is about the size of a pigeon or mallard. The feathers are soft to the touch with fine fringes which help with noise reduction when in flight.

The colouring of this medium-sized owl is very individual and variations from tawny brown rufous-coloured birds, through to grey-brown are found. These variations in colour are

The famous staccato call of the tawny owl 'woooo-woo-wo-wo-wo-woooo' is generally used exclusively by the male.

called phases or morphs and the grey phase is usually characterised by a lighter facial disk. Both phases have flecks, bars and streaks of many subtle shades of brown through to white on the back, making it easily camouflaged when in its favourite dappled light woodland. Deep dark eyes are common to both phases as are; no ear tufts, a soft olivey horn-coloured bill and legs feathered in white or buff. The colour is very irregular and this makes the tawny very hard to see when roosting in trees during daylight hours.

Although some variations in colour can be found across many parts of Europe, the UK tawny population is 'geographically defined' by the fact that we are an island and that tawnys are sedentary birds who are not keen to cross water. Gradually, over time,

this isolation from mainland Europe (and even a variation between the north and south of the UK) would seem to indicate the possibility that a new subspecies is being formed. Research continues.

The famous staccato call of the tawny owl 'woooo-woo-wo-wo-wo-woooo' is generally used exclusively by the male; the female using the equally famous 'ke-wick' light screech, although males will use that too. A territory-setting tool, the calls can be heard in late summer and through the autumn. It is also used in courtship and, when the female is brooding the eggs, as a preface to the arrival of food. It becomes almost a duet, with the 'ke-wick' from the hungry female being answered with the 'too-whit' from the male, followed shortly by the arrival of prey and a reprise of the 'too-whit'. This heralding of food is used by parents with their owlets, the latter answering with cheeping calls. In the past it has generally been understood that owls only call at night. However, in the UK it would seem that tawnies do in fact call on a regular basis during the hours of daylight too. A study in 2013 showed that calling was most prevalent between 9:00am and 3:00pm with a midday peak, this occurring mainly in the south of England and in bright sunshine. There is no similar daylight calling amongst tawnies in Europe, with only one or two pockets of this behaviour being recorded. Research continues.

The eyes of the tawny owl are very large; it has been estimated that if our eyes were proportionally as large they would be the size of tennis balls! They have very good binocular vision compared to most other diurnal hunters. They do not move or roll the eyes but can instead rotate the head through 270 degrees in both directions and up and down. This is facilitated by having a very long neck, as can be seen on the skeleton on page 11.

Like all owls, the tawny has ears which are slightly offset, with one higher than the other. Sound is collected on two planes through the feathers of the slightly dished 'facial mask', the feathers being specially adapted to allow sound through.

The slightly smaller, lower, downward-tilting left ear more easily collects sounds from below, thus offering pinpoint accuracy when hunting in darkness. The ears are also very sensitive to low frequency sounds. It can be well imagined that, to an animal with such acute hearing, the patter of rain on the leaves in woodland would cause a real problem when hunting prey in the undergrowth. This is certainly one of the issues that must contribute to owl starvation in drawn

The territory of a tawny owl, once fixed by a monogamous pair, remains constant throughout their lives together.

out periods of wet weather.

The territory of a tawny owl, once fixed by a monogamous pair (very occasionally males are polygamous), remains constant throughout their lives together. The spread of the territory through deciduous mixed woodland is not large and consequently they get to know it very well, retaining an extensive memory of where to find prey and good roosting spots which they change regularly. They are aggressively territorial and many young owls starve to death when they are unable to find a new territory on leaving the nest in the autumn.

The tawny owl hunts mainly at night, the exception being when the male is feeding the female and young in the nest. It has slightly shorter wings than other owls, making it very manoeuvrable in woodland but, owing to its stockier build, slow on take-off. Whilst using agile wing beats amongst trees it will, like the barn owl, glide silently over open ground.

It regurgitates pellets after swallowing prey whole; these are usually between 3 and 7cm long, grey in colour and rather loose in appearance. By inspecting the pellets, we have a very clear picture of what they eat and, surprisingly, the urban tawny has a different diet to the rural bird.

In the rural environment, the tawny will perch relatively close to the ground waiting for passing prey. This it will pounce on with amazing speed and in almost total silence because of the fringed flight feathers on the edge

of its wings. The powerful claws of a tawny will dispatch prey with one stroke. The rural diet is mainly rats, mice, voles, shrews, bats and a small percentage (10%) of birds. It will also take worms and insects and even frogs and fish if needs must. This rather omnivorous attitude has no doubt helped it survive where others, like the barn owl, have struggled. However, like the barn owl it is susceptible to 'bad' years for rodents which can have a devastating effect on numbers of young surviving their first year.

In the urban landscape, the percentage of rodents and similar prey drops considerably and the diet is almost exclusively birds. Using rooftops and telegraph poles as viewing posts over gardens, cemeteries and parkland, they will take sparrows, starlings, thrushes and blackbirds from their roosts. Tawnies have been known to take smaller owls too, the little owl being an obvious target, and it is also recorded that they will beat along hedges with their wings to flush out smaller birds.

Natural predators of the tawny include common buzzard, eagle owl, pine marten and fox. In recent years avian malaria has been found more widely in tawnies, the increase almost certainly caused by a rise in global temperatures. Interestingly it does not always prove fatal and the birds seem to build a resistance to it. Fatalities caused by man usually involve vehicles or trains. The tawny owl can breed at a year and they usually survive for about five years. The oldest wild bird recorded was eighteen years old and a captive tawny lived for twenty seven years, but this is exceptional.

Fights for nesting territory can run from October to November of the year before a pair will raise owlets; the male defining the territory, the female

The owlets can fly at five weeks but may be dependant on the male and female for food for up to three months after leaving the nest.

the nest site. During the winter, the pair will roost together and form a firm bond if it is a new pairing. The tawny nest is, like other owls', not 'built' as such; they are quite happy to use a hole or strong fork in a tree or take over the abandoned nest of another bird (crow, magpie, raven) or even an old squirrel drey.

There will be only one brood a year and the almost round, pure white eggs are laid at intervals of anything up to a week any time from the end of March. Having laid the eggs sequentially, the female then does all the incubation for approximately thirty days, the male bringing her food. The subsequent hatching takes some time and the eventual full brood will all be of different ages. The male alone feeds both female

and owlets until they are all hatched. The owlets remain in the nest or environs for a further month and a half, being fed by both parents.

The owlets can fly at five weeks but may be dependant on the male and female for food for up to three months after leaving the nest. Eventually, having learnt to fend for themselves they will disperse to find new territories of their own. Tawny owls are very fierce defenders of their nesting territories. They will use threatening behaviour to other birds and will take on cats, dogs and foxes who might come too close to the nest. Famously in 1937, the subsequently world-famous bird photographer Eric Hosking, who was then only 28, lost his left eye to a tawny owl when he was returning

to his photographic hide at night.
Females are not afraid to defend
owlets from any human coming too
close and it is also well documented
that bird ringers will wear hard
hats and visors when dealing with
tawnies.

Long-Eared Owl

Long-Eared Owl

Family *strigidae*

Genus *asio*

Latin Name *asio otus*

Common Name long-eared owl

Length 28–40cm

Wing span approx 90–105cm
Females generally 5–10% longer
than males

Weight 200–400g
Females generally 20–40%
heavier than males

The 'professorial' long-eared owl, with its glaring orange eyes and frowning demeanour, wears an almost constantly furious expression. However, being a very well-camouflaged bird of woodland, particularly coniferous woodland, it is rather shy and not much heard (predominantly only in the breeding season) and even more rarely seen as it is a fully nocturnal hunter. It has a habit during daytime roosting of sitting very still, hunkered close to the trunk of the tree with its feathers drawn in, or even fluffed out as it thinks fit and blending with the texture of the bark. All of which makes it perhaps the UK's most under-recorded bird.

It can be imagined that numbers of this wary camouflage expert are hard to estimate, particularly when you consider that any population in mid-winter (the time when they might be most clearly seen) will be increased by Scandinavian and other European migratory long-ears, to say nothing of UK birds flying down from the north to overwinter in the south. Approximate figures in 2016 indicate 3,500 breeding pairs.

The eyes are always a very bright orange but the plumage varies considerably.

Although it can look larger in flight, the long-eared owl is in fact comparable in size to a wood pigeon. Slightly smaller than the tawny owl and slimmer too, it has long feather 'ear' tufts that it raises when alarmed or threatened. The eyes are always a very bright orange but the plumage varies considerably, predominantly a slightly tawny, greyish hue overall with many flecks and dabs of darker brown. When in flight, there is a russet wash of colour under the wings. The facial disk is rich fawn, marked with a slightly paler edge and a thin darker line, and a 'ruff' of feathers down the centre of the face that can be brought over the beak to hide it. The legs and feet are feathered.

As with other owls, the facial disk plays its part in capturing sound and that, combined with ear openings at different heights, gives it pinpoint accuracy when finding prey in anything up to and including total darkness. These hearing attributes are matched in other owls but it would seem that the long-eared owl has one very specific extra aid to sound gathering. It is possible that the muscles used to raise and lower the 'ear' tufts also work to change the shape of the ear openings, thus increasing the information gathered; not really 'ears' but helping the owl to hear.

The natural habitat of the long-eared owl is woodland, small copses and wooded areas on the edge of open countryside. It does have a preference for conifers and, whilst not favouring the centre of dense woodland, thick woods planted with 20m wide 'rides' offer a hunting strip for them to glide silently down. The silent glide

is common to other owl species but the long-eared owl is also master of the silent flap and that, combined with its manoeuvrability in woodland, makes it a formidable hunter. Safe roosting places close to an open hunting area are vital. The winter is a time when one of the long-eared owl's most unusual traits is seen; that of communal roosting. This involves many owls, anything up to fifty or more birds coming together to roost and is known as a 'parliament' of owls. Loose roosting groups like this will use the same sites year after year, possibly including the same birds. These parliaments are not seen as frequently as they were in the

past and it is suggested that global warming has dissuaded continental owls from making the North Sea crossing now that home areas are as warm as migration sites in the winter.

The long-eared owl is found across the UK, apart from the south-west of England. Those birds that breed in the north of Scotland will migrate south for the winter. The call of the male long-eared owl is rather like the sound made by blowing over the top of a bottle; the female call has a more rasping note to add to that 'hoo

Feeding mainly on mice and voles and other small mammals, they will take a higher proportion of small birds during the winter when they will snatch them from roosting perches. (This appears to apply only to UK residents and there are apocryphal stories of them beating bushes with their wings to flush out sleeping birds, mainly house sparrows.) The hunting does not take place in the woodland that they favour during the day but they will be found from dusk until dawn zig-zagging low to the ground over open fields, with a slightly tilted head to catch the sound of prey moving below. Pellets are produced, as with other owls, usually three to four hours after feeding.

Like other owls, long-eared owl numbers are cyclical, based on the numbers of small mammals available during the breeding period. Any decline in numbers may also be linked to an increase in tawny owls; they have been known to predate the

hoo' sound. There is also a shriek-like alarm call for both. Calling is almost always at night and usually only during the breeding season.

long-eared owl and in areas where tawny numbers are low, long-eared owl populations are stable, which suggests there may be a correlation.

Like other UK owl species, this owl is happy with a second-hand nest, abandoned crows' and magpie nests are a particular favourite. In fact, to protect long-eared owls, farmers have been advised to check for

fresh occupancy before shooting out seemingly empty nests which they do to control corvid numbers. The owls are prepared to adapt if no empty nests are available and will even nest in dense shrubs on marsh/sand-dunes or tree hollows. In extremis, they have been known to nest on the ground. (Baskets are sometimes recommended as 'nest boxes' for long-eared owls.) Males select and stake the nesting territory first and it may be one they know well but the actual nest site is not necessarily the same every year. The main feature of any pairing display is that the wings are 'clapped' from a perch before launching into a display flight.

The number of eggs laid is dependent on food sources and, as with other species, eggs are laid progressively and the female does most of the incubation whilst being fed by the male. The glossy white eggs are laid from March to June, anything from three to seven in total and are incubated for between twenty-five and twenty-eight days. The owlets leave the nest at approximately eighteen to twenty-five days and are fledged at around thirty. The young are fed for up to two months after fledging and this is when they will use the easily recognised 'squeaky gate' call to attract their parents' attention. There

is usually only a single brood but a second has been recorded in years when food is plentiful.

Long-eared owls are fierce when alarmed or when defending their nests. They make themselves as big as possible by spreading their wing feathers wide into a semi-circle around the body and lowering the head whilst hissing loudly. This display makes them appear two or three times bigger than they are. If this and the usual feigned injury tricks deployed by most animals don't work, they will actually attack with their vicious talons. Even the owlets in the nest will spread their wings if they feel threatened. Although fierce, long-eared owls are successfully predated and killed by tawny owls, eagle owls and other raptors.

Short-Eared Owl

Short-Eared Owl

Family *strigidae*

Genus *asio*

Latin Name *asio flammeus*

Common Name short-eared owl

Length 34–43cm

Wing span approx 95–110cm

Females generally 5–10% longer than males

Weight 200–450g

Females generally 20–40% heavier than males

Estimated UK breeding population in 2016: 1,000–3,000 but possibly declining and therefore amber listed.

Larger that the long-eared owl and roughly the size of a tawny, the short-eared owl has longer and thinner wings than either of them. This bird, which is found across the world, is far more diurnal than any of the other UK owl species, hunting mainly during daylight hours and usually being less active once night falls. It can often be seen in its preferred habitat of open countryside, moors, marches and dunes during the day.

The typical owl perch of a fence or fence post is a favourite from which to view the prey possibilities on the ground and, in the case of the short-eared owl, this is mainly voles. It is often seen in flight, quartering low over open countryside or even sitting on the ground on a soil hummock or low rock.

They have a somewhat nomadic existence, moving on when vole numbers decline. During the early 20th century, the bird did well as grazing was replaced with woodland plantations in the uplands of Scotland and the north of England. These newly created habitats were good for short-eared owls as they fostered an increase in vole and small mammal numbers. However, gradually the trees grew, the ground vegetation died back and so did the number of rodents, and the owls moved on. When small mammals reach nuisance levels in any area there is almost always a rise in the number of short-eared owls to be found.

Solitary hunters, they may form loose groups during the winter months to include migrants from further north, mainly Scandinavia, Russia and Iceland. These migrants can usually be found in numbers around the east coast of central and southern England, particularly the fens and marshes.

The plumage is a dark brown with buff chest and a four-barred tail. The facial disk is pale beige with a white

line around it and the bright yellow eyes are ringed with black. The feathered legs are white as are the under-wings. The 'ears', as with the long-eared owl, are not for hearing and are only used as a signal, sometimes of anxiety, sometimes of aggression; they are never seen in flight.

The voice of a short-eared owl is not its greatest feature; being mainly diurnal, it might be considered that when you can be seen clearly by other birds, visual displays would have more power. There is therefore a rather spectacular air display during courting and the birds will soar together into the open sky or the male may soar alone whilst his prospective mate watches from the ground. Wings are 'clapped' below the body by the male during flight. Sounds include a 'chef-chef' when threatened and a 'boo-boo-boo'

sound made during courtship. There are a small variety of squawks and hisses when defending the nest.

When hunting, the bird has a slow gliding flight with deep wing beats, and will hover before the pounce. Prey is most often a field vole or other small mammal (rats, mice, etc.) and even small birds when offspring are being fed or if needs must through poor weather conditions. Like all owls, the short-

eared has excellent eyesight and superlative hearing, with the off-set ear holes of other species which help in locating prey.

The nest of the short-eared owl is built on the ground, usually a roughly lined scrape hidden in grasses, heather or dead reeds. The number of round white eggs laid is, as always, dependent on vole numbers; usually between four and eight but fourteen have been recorded in a vole-abundant year. The eggs, laid at two day intervals, are incubated by the female alone (who is fed by the male) and the first will hatch after approximately twenty-four to twenty-eight days. They fledge after a further twenty-six days, having sat out on the surrounding area for the previous couple of weeks. In the past it was believed that the 'couple' stayed together after the brood were gone and might even attempt a second brood if the available food allowed. However, ongoing research started in 2017 shows that nothing could be further from the truth. The research for the British Trust for Ornithology and led by John Calladine, started in Stirling in Scotland by placing solar tags on three young short-eared owls. There were two females and one male and the tracker sent a fix signal every three hours and could pin-point the bird on a map within two to three metres.

In the spring of 2018, the first female sought a mate and incubated her first clutch of eggs relatively close by in the uplands above Perth. The eggs hatched but she abandoned the chicks to the male to look after until they fledged. This he did successfully and all fledged safely. Meanwhile, the female crossed the North Sea to Norway, a fourteen-hour journey, where she paired up with another male, laid a second clutch of eggs and again abandoned them to the care of the male. The researchers at this point began to feel that this might be a normal behaviour for a short-eared owl. Then she began a circuit of the UK starting on the west coast of Ireland, taking in both Cornwall and Devon and finally ending in Norfolk, no further pairings were made during this trip. In spring 2019 the female set off from Norfolk heading again for Norway but sadly she perished in a storm over the sea.

A further three birds were tagged on the island of Arran on the south-west coast of Scotland. The single male remained on Arran whilst

one of the females flew to Durham where, in spring 2020, she paired up and laid eggs which hatched. It is not known at the time of writing if this clutch has been abandoned as before. However, the second female remained on Arran to breed. Having found a mate, she laid eggs which hatched and, forty-eight hours later, she abandoned them to the male to rear. To date there is no information about exactly where she has gone. Research continues.

Short-eared owls can be long lived in the wild, the oldest recorded reached almost 13 years. However, the ground nesting habit of this owl does make it susceptible to predation from mammals. They will defend both themselves and the nest by flying at an intruder and pulling up at the last minute to present their talons as a weapon; they are also known for using the 'broken wing' ruse to distract predators. Mammal predators will take grown birds, whilst gulls and corvids will steal eggs and small chicks.

Little Owl

Little Owl

Family *strigidae*
Genus *athene*
Latin Name *athene noctua*
Common Name little owl
Length 19–23cm
Wing span approx 55–58cm
Females generally 5–10% longer than males
Weight 96–230g
Females generally 20–40% heavier than males

The appropriately named little owl is about the size of a mistle thrush and was introduced to the UK during the 1800s. Two men are responsible for the establishment of the species in the UK: in 1874 Col. Meade-Waldo, Edenbridge, Kent, and 1889 Lord Lilford at Lilford Hall, Oundle, Northampton. (Lord Lilford's introduction was the more successful as the bird was originally known as Lilford's owl.) Within forty years the little owl could be found as far north as Yorkshire and they are now resident over the Scottish border. It would seem its successful colonisation was down to it predating mainly insects and not therefore conflicting with the native owl population. Estimated breeding pairs at 2016 were approximately 5,700, although it is felt that numbers are gradually falling, possibly due to loss of habitats and the use of insecticides which have a great impact on insect eaters.

Following fears in the mid-1930s that little owls were predating game chicks and were therefore being shot in some numbers, Alice Hibbert-Ware was asked to undertake a study of the normal diet of the little owl

(Report of The Little Owl Food Inquiry 1936–1937). To ensure scrupulous responsibility and decision making, the British Trust for Ornithology was asked to oversee the methodology. This they did and, satisfyingly for the supporters of the little owl, it was found to eat mainly mice, voles, and small birds during the breeding season and large volumes of beetles, earwigs, crane flies and worms, only occasionally did they take game bird chicks. There were, however, conservation issues with a few

offshore islands where rare seabirds were predated and in these instances the rare birds took precedence.

The strongest features of the little owl are its piercing yellow eyes and pale, creamy-white brows. The general appearance is flat-headed with a short, plump body. The colouring is grey/brown with spotted white on the back and a pale chest with grey/brown flecks. Fine feathering covers the legs and feet and the beak is a pale olivey green. Most hunting is done between dusk and dawn but they are diurnal, particularly when feeding young in the summer, when they can often be seen perched on fence posts, tree stumps or exposed branches staring at the ground, surveying for potential prey which they will drop down onto.

They fly with a swooping habit, not unlike a woodpecker or mistle thrush but quite different from any other owl. They predate insects and small mammals, and are therefore often seen running on the ground with a determined march-like step. When unsettled, another trait is a bobbing head movement alternating with a side-to-side action.

They are noisy birds and have over twenty different calls, an almost wheezy 'kee-ew' being the most often quoted, particularly during the breeding season (March to early May) although there is also a much heard sort of 'whoop'. The calls are not much like other owls and it could be supposed that this is because their bodies, being smaller, have little resonance. They have very good eyesight with an ability similar to diurnal raptors, as you would expect from a bird who is a day and night hunter. Like all owls, their hearing is exceptional.

They favour a territory of mixed habitats – open countryside, hedgerows, parkland and farmland and will live around small villages and farm buildings too. The life-long pairs will live in the chosen territory throughout the breeding year.

Little owls, as already discussed, have a varied diet which broadens during the breeding season to include small birds and, during periods of rain, earthworms can become an offering to the young too. Whatever is available seems to be the main drive for the little owl as, once the owlets are hatched, they

hunt for food all day long. Little owls are important in our own economic cycle as they can control pest populations in crops.

Like other owls, the little owl shuns the need to build a serious nest and is also an opportunist in using small tree holes, holes in walls, nest boxes and even unoccupied rabbit burrows.

Three to five small matt white eggs are laid sequentially from mid-April to May. They are incubated mainly by the female for twenty-eight to twenty-nine days, with feeding by both parents being required for a another twenty-eight days (approximately), at which point the owlets will gradually leave the nest to sit out on branches close by.

Both parents will continue to feed them until late summer when the youngsters will leave to find their own territories. Sometimes, weather and prey permitting, there will be a second brood.

The main threat to the little owl are foxes, stoats, pine martens and other owls and raptors as well as domestic cats and dogs. They will call to warn others that predators are near and will hide; their colouring working as a good camouflage. On the back of their heads, they have a V of pale feathers that, when given a quick glance, looks like eyes, thus warning off any predator coming from behind.

Snowy Owl

Snowy Owl

Family *strigidae*
Genus *nyctea/bubo*
Latin Name *nyctea scandiaca/ bubo scandiaca*
Common Name snowy owl

Originally of the genus *nyctea scandiaca* but DNA profiling shows it to be closer to the genus *bubo*. This is still a matter of debate so both are shown here.

Length 53–66cm
Wing span approx 135–165cm
Females generally 5–10% longer than males
Weight 1.1–2kg
Females generally 20–40% heavier than males

The nomadic snowy owl is a large bird, the males being mainly white, whilst the females have brown/dark grey flecking on the back and head. Eyes are golden and the beak and talons are black.

In its natural Arctic habitat it will feed mainly on lemmings and voles but it is an opportunistic feeder and will take almost anything as needs must, including fish, other smaller birds and carrion. Very susceptible to fluctuation in food stocks, if lemming numbers crash they will move farther south. This is undoubtedly why, between 1967 and 1975 they were to be found on Fetlar in the Shetland Isles of Scotland. During this period, twenty-one owlets were raised by a breeding pair (there was another female who laid eggs but none hatched). However, the male did not return in 1976, the two females summered there in the years following but there was no further breeding without the male.

In the early 2000s, a male and female appeared on North Uist but did not breed. Early March 2013 saw a rare sighting in the Cairngorms and the Scottish Wildlife Trust has stated that a sighting once a year is usual.

Snowy owls are ground nesters and make a scrape, filled loosely with grass and feathers. As with other owls, the eggs are laid sequentially and incubated by the female. The number of eggs is dependent on food availability and is usually between three and seven but could be up to fourteen in a good year with a plentiful supply of lemmings. Owlets leave the nest at about twenty-five days but are not fledged until forty to sixty days and both parents will fully feed until they are.

Now classed as a 'rare visitor' to the UK, you are only likely to get a sighting of this magnificent owl in the Harry Potter films, where his owl Hedwig is a snowy.

Eagle Owl

Eagle Owl

Family *strigidae*
Genus *bubo*
Latin Name *bubo bubo*
Common Name eagle owl
Length 66–71cms
Wing span approx 90–105cm
Females generally 5–10% longer than males
Weight 2.7–4kg
Females generally 20–40% heavier than males

With its superior size, bright orange eyes and large ear tufts, the eagle owl is an intimidating presence. A generally buff/tawny-coloured bird with brown flecks, starting with large ones around the neck and down the back but thinning down over the chest to finer, more delicate lines. The pale facial disk is oval rather than circular and the ear tufts are thick above the centre of the eyes. The talons and beak are dark grey/black.

They are formidable silent hunters, both nocturnally and diurnally, and will take mammals from the ground or birds in flight or at roost. They will eat almost anything from bugs to roe deer fawns as well as fish, frogs and crabs. The favourite staple mammals are voles, rats, mice, foxes, hares and rabbits, with crows, partridge, buzzard and seabirds amongst the bird population. Pellets are large, as you would expect, at 75 x 32mm.

During late winter, and having chosen a ground scrape to nest in amongst rocks or in open woodland, the female lays one to four eggs. The eagle owl, like other native species, lays the eggs sequentially, and the female will incubate them for between thirty-one and thirty-six days, being fed by the male during this period. Once fledged, the chicks will be supported by the parents for about twenty to twenty-four weeks and will be looking for their own territories by the autumn. The eagle owl has no natural predators in the UK and mortality is usually caused by electrocution, traffic collisions or shooting.

Like the snowy owl there are issues about whether an eagle owl should be considered a native species now that there are breeding pairs in small pockets of the country. If you compare the statistics at the beginning of each species chapter, you will see that both eagle and snowy owls are considerably larger than other UK owls. They are intimidating predators requiring a large territory as they scare off other birds.

Nobody is currently saying exactly how may eagle owls there are in the UK (somewhere between twelve and forty pairs has been suggested) but it would seem that small cohorts of escapees/released birds are breeding and beginning to make waves amongst conservation groups; one side saying they should be culled to protect native birds and the other side saying they were once native and should therefore be allowed to re-establish themselves. (There is fossil evidence that they were present here 9,000 years ago.)

An experienced falconer says about the issue: 'There are eagle owl populations from escapees occurring where there are also hen harriers. The government did a risk assessment and concluded that increasing numbers could be a threat to other red list birds including hen

harriers. It is noteworthy that there would not be an issue if hen harriers were not so badly persecuted that numbers are disgracefully low and they are unable to breed effectively. In the argument about whether eagle owls should have native status or not, (bearing in mind little owls are an introduced species but nobody minds them!) I consider, in theory, eagle owls should have native status. I've kept, flown, cared for and rehabilitated every UK species... the eagle owl is one of the few birds of prey that are hand-reared for flying purposes as they're easily stressed and hand-reared birds cope better.' Debate continues.

The Suffolk Owl Sanctuary

Established as a registered charity in 2001, the Suffolk Owl Sanctuary is based at Stonham Aspal in Suffolk, where it operates a comprehensive facility for the care and rehabilitation of owls from the region and the promotion of owl conservation throughout the UK and beyond.

The Sanctuary is open to the public all year round, where it maintains the following services as the beneficiary of public donations.

A raptor hospital for injured wild owls and other birds of prey

The Owl and Raptor Hospital at S.O.S. is fully equipped for the care and treatment of the many injured wild owls and other birds of prey which are brought into the Sanctuary every year. Many of these can be given a recuperative overnight pick-me-up before being re-released back to the wild shortly afterwards.

Flight recovery aviaries for recuperating wild owls

Owls that are more seriously injured but stand a good chance of mid to long-term recovery are given medical aid and sometimes surgery, and are then allowed the space and time to recuperate fully in one of the secluded flight recovery aviaries at the Sanctuary before returning to the wild. Regrettably, injured owls that are brought into the Sanctuary but are professionally judged to

be beyond the pale, with no hope of meaningful quality of life, are euthanased by a vet.

A hack-back team which safely introduces recovered owls back to the wild

S.O.S. also receives a number of nestlings and these require specialised handling from the Hack-Back team, who also manage the careful rehabilitation of birds who have been at the Sanctuary for a long period of time recuperating. A temporary hack box (an enlarged nest box with a mesh-covered outdoor area) is sited in a suitable location from where these birds will gradually be reintroduced back to their natural environment.

Owl education visits to schools and colleges

Giving talks and setting projects for schools, agricultural colleges and disenfranchised groups who either visit the Sanctuary or to whom we out-reach, is the focus of our Education Team and the Wise Owl Roadshow for Schools. We also consult with landowners and farmers with advice for those interested in developing suitable habitat or nesting locations for owls in the wild.

A nestbox scheme which builds and maintains new habitat for wild owls

One of the most important spheres of operation for the Sanctuary is the S.O.S. Wild Owl Nest Box Scheme. This includes the time-consuming search for suitable locations for man-made nest boxes (the availability of proper habitat and sufficient natural prey species being the chief determining factors); the building and secure erection of nest boxes made from safe, long-lasting, environmentally friendly materials; and the careful monitoring of nesting activity within the boxes that form part of the network.

Free information and advice on owl care and conservation

The Information and Advice Centre is open every day of the year except at Christmas. During summer months demonstrations featuring owls in flight are given with commentaries which inform visitors about the lifestyles, habitats and conservation status of British owls and other birds of prey.

Extending the reach of information and advice about owls beyond the confines of the Sanctuary is covered through the publication of various freely-available leaflets on specific and general related topics. In recent years the round-the-clock manning of a Q-and-A website at www.owl-help.org.uk offers immediate qualified response to

enquiries from around the world – last year, over 1000 e-mail questions about owls, their care and conservation from as far afield as Alaska!

Heather's Story
#owlmummy

This first picture is the beginning of my story of the five baby little owls that I rescued from a nest that had been dug out by a fox... who had killed the parents. I had no idea they were nesting so close to the house and one day in May 2015 I woke to find two dead adults on the lawn.

I only guessed what happened but searched high and low in the tree stump and found five two-day-old owlets, which I subsequently rushed over to the wonderful Maz at the Suffolk Owl Sanctuary, who admitted she had never raised any so young before but said she would have a go.

Maz took them home at night to keep them fed, and returned them to me when they were big enough to be 'hacked on', this is basically a nest box which is housed in the woods here and I would feed them with mice daily until they were ready to go it alone.

Of course, once Maz realised I was up for it and prepared to deal with frozen mice, the flood gates opened. Gradually, she would bring me more and more, including tawnys.

We only lost one, which was too damaged when it grew and could not take off. I think in total I have raised fourteen little owls and five tawnys thus far; that is one heck of a lot of mice – in fact I had to get another freezer just for the mice! We feed them dark mice and not white so they know what to look for in the wild.

The rot set in when Maz visited here; up to that point she did not realise I had so much woodland. It was a natural progression for her to ask if I would be prepared to bring on the owlets. It helps to bring in new stock too so that my little family did not interbreed, the gene pool spread rather than contracted.

I have this wonderful fairy ring in the middle of woodland which is utterly private and this is where I rear them. I mow the grass so it is short and then they can feed on snails and slugs etc. when I'm not feeding them mice.

I have several little families, which of course don't do well if it is too wet as owls hate the wet; cold they can cope with but wet AND cold does for them.

I got the chap who helps me with the strimming to make me hacking boxes of my own so Maz can bring owls over if need be without having to the find a box to bring with her. Of course I always have mice in the freezer much like you would have peas!!

In these pictures I am teaching them to feed and fly, just call me Ms. Doolittle.

I ended up having to wear a hat as they would try and land on my head!!

Of course they could do me some damage and I heard of one person losing an eye by accident as the owl flew to greet him. There is a fine line between these hunting birds and keeping them wild but tame enough to feed and rear.

Above: Waiting rather like Oliver for me to feed it.

Above: It's unusual to get a sleeping tawny picture, but this one trusted me and just dozed beside me.

The poorly one I reared had a leg that had been damaged at birth, so the vet would not let me keep it here. He said it would never hunt as it could not run to lift off; that was a very sad day. I reared it in the cart lodge with logs etc. and it would feed from my hand – but it was not to be.

I am so pleased to be able to tell my story. What I want to do at some point is raise enough money for another incubator. The Suffolk Owl Sanctuary can get a lot of owlets in at the same time and have nowhere to rear them, particularly May/June time.

If you feel like donating to Suffolk Owl Sanctuary please go to their website giving page at owlbarn. charitycheckout.co.uk/donate

The Owl in Myth and Legend

In 1994 three caves were discovered in Chauvet, France which contained the oldest image of an owl, approximately 30,000 years old.

Owls are very important characters in myth and legend, it would be easy to fill a whole book, let alone a chapter about them. Therefore, please consider this to be something of a taster intended to whet your enthusiasm for this most fascinating of birds.

The oldest fossil remains of an owl are 60 million years old; not surprisingly this makes them one of the oldest groups of birds in the world. In 1994 three caves were discovered in Chauvet, France which contained the oldest image of an owl, approximately 30,000 years old.

In ancient Egyptian hieroglyphs, all birds and animals are shown in profile with the exception of the owl whose body is in profile but whose head is turned and looking at the reader. Owls were not revered by the Egyptians as other birds were, but they were respected and therefore occasionally mummified. From these mummies we know the barn owl was present in ancient Egypt.

The Greeks worshipped the goddess Athene (sometimes Athena) and her sacred totem was the owl. Her original choice was a crow but she found him too mischievous and was taken with the solemn gravity and wisdom of the owl. It was considered very good luck and an omen of forthcoming victory to see an owl prior to battle, so much so that one general had a caged owl amongst his baggage, to release and raise morale before the start of battle.

'There goes an owl' was a phrase used to mean 'there are signs of victory'. Romans, however, believed the exact opposite. Seeing an owl meant impending defeat and perhaps this is the biggest dichotomy of the owl; as many cultures seem to love it as hate it.

From approximately the sixth to the first centuries BC, an Athenian tetradrachm coin showed the goddess on one side and an owl (thought to be a little owl) on the other. Colloquially, the tetradrachm was known as an 'owl' and even today the Greek Euro has an owl at its centre. (President Theodore Roosevelt at the beginning of the twentieth century was so taken with Greek 'owls' that he carried one in his pocket. He thought that US coinage was artistically dull and ugly and worked hard to develop something as beautiful as the 'owl'.

THE FIGURE ABOVE
IS THAT OF MINERVA
GODDESS OF WISDOM
AND OF DRAMA BY
JOHN WOLSTENHOLME
1801

His pet plan failed, however, when it was found that the design by Augustus Saint-Gaudens for a $20 gold coin, although beautiful, took nine pressings to execute and was therefore unfit for mass production. Only twenty-four were ever made.)

The Romans, on defeating the Greek armies, adopted the goddess Athene who became their goddess of wisdom, Minerva. The owl remained as her symbol but the Romans feared the owl as the harbinger of death and were inclined to kill it and nail it to the door as a talisman of safety for the house. A daylight sighting or calling was considered a particularly bad omen. Thought to be the messengers of sorcerers, body parts of owls were used in their mystical, magical practices. (This is also a belief amongst Zulus and other groups in West Africa.)

In ancient China during the Shang Dynasty (c. 1500–1045BC) bronze wine jars were made in the shape of owls. It is not recorded what the stocky owl figures with their head lids were for, but it is possible they were part of the Chinese ceremony of ancestor worship. The weight of the figures alone would suggest they were made for people of some status. Perhaps they were buried with the body to provide 'sight' in the dark journey to the other world? In this period the owl might be thought helpful and benign but by the Taoist era (c. 220BC–AD265) his predatory nature had come to the fore and a monster character had evolved; owlets being thought to cannibalise their mother. The Taoist religion has a part-owl, part-man god, Lei-gong the God of Thunder; with the top half owl and bottom half man he punished men for their secret crimes.

The native Ainu people of Hokkaido in Japan revere the owl as *kotankor kamuy* a god of the land and plenty who will look after and help all the humans under his care.

The Indian goddess Lakshmi, when by herself, travels on an owl; if she is

with Vishnu then they travel together on the eagle Garuda. Talismans are made from owl bones, beaks and talons. The direct method of improving your eyes; in Indian folklore is to eat owl eyes, this is an idea prevalent with medicine men in Africa also.

Generally, African mythology has the owls in the 'bad' role; they are associated with evil and as such should be killed at every opportunity. Witch-bird is the 'pidgin' English for owl and Cameroonians can't even bear to give it a name and call it only 'the bird that makes you afraid'.

The owl is an important figure to Native American Indians who have many owl myths; as we have seen in other times and cultures, sometimes good, sometimes evil. Harbinger of sickness or death in several tribes, message carrier from beyond the grave or the souls of the departed in others; the bad spirit with which to threaten naughty children or the incarnation of a god and to be treated with respect. The Cherokee nation, for instance, thinks of the owl as the ultimate in sacred purity (the cougar and the owl being the only animals to stay awake during the seven days of creation, thus designating themselves nocturnal). The human characteristics of the owl with its

The owl is an important figure to Native American Indians who have many owl myths; sometimes good, sometimes evil.

'face' make it sacred and revered for its insight and understanding of the human condition.

Some tribes thought of owls as 'witches' that had shape-shifted into the form of an owl. It was hard for the average tribe members to differentiate between a 'real' owl and a 'witch owl' so it was thought safer to avoid owls altogether. Of course medicine men and holy people had special understanding of these things and could tell the difference.

Found owl feathers can be used in several ways; placed in a child's crib to keep it safe from evil as the Zuni tribe believed, or they might be hung in a doorway to ward off illness as some tribes thought the owl to be the bringer of health.

The clan of the owl is also present in Native American cultures: the Hopi, Tlingit and Mohave tribes all have owl clans and the bird can often be found as the top effigy on a totem pole.

The 'Spedis Owl' is a petroglyph made thousands of years ago by ancient Indian civilisations. Petroglyphs are powerful symbols carved, scratched or ground straight onto rock surface. Originally noted in 1873, and finally surveyed in the archeological sense in 1983, Spedis Owls are found thoughout the Wind River country of Wyoming. No one tribe is thought to be responsible for these images with at least six tribes being known to use them.

The Spedis Owl (below) was found in 1956 as the Dalles Dam was about to flood the area. This piece is thought to either act as a safeguard against water devils that could rise up and drag you into the deep and/or an indication of ownership of a fishing spot. We will probably never know.

The Dakota Hidatsa people held the burrowing owl to be a guardian spirit for warriors, whilst the Hopi held it as sacred and; their 'god of the dead' and guardian of the underworld. Not surprisingly, the fact that these owls live underground indicates that they had much to do with the area beneath the soil and look after the health of seeds and plants too. The Screech Owl Dance and the Horned Owl Dance are both part of the tribal dance culture of the Creek Indians, with ceremonial songs to go with them.

There are many tales concerning owls in the Native American Indian oral tradition. Here is just one, related to a story collector in 1905.

The Hunter and the Owl concerns a hunter who leaves his village with his wife and goes on a hunting trip. After several days they have found no game and are sitting by the camp fire in the evening when they hear an owl hoot, followed by a laugh. A good omen was read into this and so the hunter searches and finds the tree where the owl is perched. Calling the owl 'Mo-hoo-mus' (grandfather) he explains how he has had no luck hunting and if the owl will send game his way, both game to eat and game with fur that he may take home a bountiful hoard, he will take the fat and the heart from the biggest deer (an owl favourite) and hang it in a tree for the owl to feast on. The owl laughs again and the hunter takes it that a contract has been struck.

The next day, just before daybreak, the hunter leaves the camp, armed with his bow and arrows. In no time at all a very large buck deer is killed. He forgets his promise to the owl to hang up the fat and the heart and hurries towards the camp with the deer; hoping to make another foray before it gets fully light. He carries the deer across his back and it truly is a big beast and he has to stop and rest. Then he hears the owl hoot, there is no laugh to follow as there was before. The owl is not happy.

The owl flies down and hovers low before the man and curses him for forgetting their agreement. 'When you put the deer down you will fall down dead.' it tells him. The hunter agrees that he has been remiss in not keeping his promise but he too has power to curse and says 'You cannot keep in the air forever, when you alight you will fall down dead. Let us see which of us is the stronger!!'

The owl circles and begins to feel tired too and comes back to the hunter. 'Let us each withdraw our curses as this situation is bad for both of us. Let us be friends from now on.' The hunter agrees and immediately puts down the carcass and cuts out the heart and heart fat and hangs it up for the owl.

During the next few days the hunter and his wife worked hard catching and preparing all the game that came their way and returned to their village laden with the owl's bounty. A hard lesson had been well learnt, 'never forget a promise made.'

There are several old Inuit tales involving the owl. In some variants of the story, the owl and the raven make clothes for each other but this is my favourite, with the birds painting one another. Both birds at this time were a simple white and, being bored, one day decide to paint each other with black lamp oil. The raven goes first and makes a really good job of the

owl, lovely brush strokes over her breast and then dark wings flecked with white. The owl is delighted, so much so that she gives the raven a new pair of Inuit kamiks (boots). Now it is the owl's turn to paint the raven, but the excited raven just wants to parade around in her new kamiks and will not stand still. The owl in exasperation, throws the lamp oil over the raven... who has been shiny black ever since! (This story can be seen in a delightful stop frame animation using life-like seal fur puppets by Co Hoedeman, well worth searching for on YouTube.)

A Polish myth has girls who die unmarried being turned into doves, whilst those who are married become owls. Furthermore, owls are nocturnal because they are so beautiful that other birds will be

jealous and mob them if they come out during the day.

The barn owl is often centre stage in English folklore, with a menacing and gloomy reputation, almost always spoken of in terms of death, very much the spirit of darkness, a literary 'bird of doom'. The usual dichotomy applies; on the one hand sacred to the Celts with mystic powers, and in the North, to hear it call was good luck, but conversely the call of an owl close to a sickroom window meant death would follow close behind.

The prize for the most bizarre myth concerning owls must be an old English one. This states that if you walk around a tree on which an owl is sitting it will strangle itself as it tries to follow you by turning its head! The weather could be predicted by barn owls; screeching meant cold weather or a storm, however, all options were kept open as an owl heard during bad weather also meant a change was coming. One wonders if the 'nailing an owl to a barn door' custom to ward off evil was brought to England by the Romans (as already mentioned), they believed in this too. Raw owl eggs were thought to be a cure for drunkenness, whilst eyesight could be restored with a potion made from the ashes of cooked owls eggs. Owl broth was used to aid children with whooping-cough (though it's not clear if this comprised the actual owl or its eggs).

Celtic folklore calls the owl *cailleach-oidhche* in Gaelic and it is usually seen as the bringer of truth and wisdom, with barn owls especially being able to 'see the hidden and hear the unspoken'. Not surprisingly, the owl is often portrayed as the Underworld guide, able to see in darkness, one who will unmask those who deceive the good-hearted. Pieces of a bronze cauldron found on Brå in Jutland dating from the 3rd century BC, when reassembled bore the image of several owls (and bulls) around its one metre diameter. It now forms part of the collection at the Moesgård Museum in Denmark.

The owl is thought by some scholars to be a sacred animal to the Cult of the Head, the Celtic pan-European group that took heads as totems in battle. Whilst acknowledging that the head was the most important part of the body to these people, research continues as to whether they were truly 'head hunters', but the owl is definitely represented along with rams and bulls in this strange cult. The owl has also been linked with a Celtic fertility goddess.

In Welsh mythology, as in other cultures, the owl is the creature of death but wisdom too. After shapeshifting into a powerful owl the goddess Arianrhod can see into the human soul and subconscious with her huge owl eyes. The dead are lifted by her to the place of the dead – the moon – and her palace is Caer Arianrhod (the Aurora Borealis). It is said that her wings bring comfort and solace to those who search for her. Perhaps the most important

Welsh myth concerning owls is that of the beautiful Blodeuwedd. A modern reworking of this tale by Jackie Morris follows this chapter.

The making of modern day myths

In June we went camping in Devon with our grandchildren. As is the way of these things, the loo was quite a way from the tent and I often found myself walking back through a row of cherry trees at all times of day and in all light conditions.

The first one I noticed was so obvious it made me jump. My goodness, here was a tree with an owl's face in it. Was I thinking about owls so much because of my research and writing that I had started 'seeing' them in everything?

Time passed. I am strolling to the loo again and this time, higher up the same tree I see an owl in profile.

This is getting really creepy now and I have started scrutinising all the other trees for signs of owls. There are none; just this one tree. Finally, the day before we leave, on the other side of the same tree I see another one.

I am so chilled by this that I get my husband to look. I have not said anything up until now but really, is this me going very slightly mad? No, he assures me, he can see at least two of my three owls; he finds the one in profile the hardest but eventually he gets that one too.

I started thinking about how this might have played out in medieval times. Would this have made the tree 'special'? Would locals have started visiting it if they had needed help with problems? Suddenly I could understand the draw of the representation of a live animal as a totem, a spot for contemplation, a place of response.

When we left the campsite, I have to admit I went and said goodbye to the owl tree. It seemed the polite thing to do.

ANIMAL WATCH

The owls are not what they seem

ARLINGTON, North Military Road, 3000 block, 5:20 p.m. Nov. 10. Responding to a call about an injured owl on the side of the road, an officer found a large mushroom.

Among cases reported by the Animal Welfare League of Arlington.

Blodeuwedd
by Jackie Morris

Preface

It feels as if some stories have been known to me my whole life, ingrained in my DNA. And indeed I have lived with the story of Blodeuwedd for some forty years now, when I first heard of her in The Owl Service *by Alan Garner.*

Later, living in Wales, I learned of her origins in The Mabinogion.

Lleu was cursed. He could have no mortal woman to be his wife. So Math and Gwyddion made him a woman from meadowsweet, oak flowers and gorse. And she was perfect for him in every way.

But she fell in love with another, Gronw Pebr. Together they plotted to kill her husband.

For punishment, Math turned her into an owl.

This story has flown through my dreams and paintings. But one man's curse can be another woman's blessing.

Jackie Morris

Blodeuwedd

He did not ask permission, either of my selves, nor of the wild gods, when he tore me from the mountain's side and wove his spells to bind broom and meadowsweet and the flowers of oak, and shape them into woman.

He knew nothing of how ancient I was, nor how beneath the earth we connected, spoke, in a slow chemical language of green, connected in ways he could not begin to imagine.

He neither understood nor cared that I left behind me so many of my children.

He made me woman, skin meadowsweet cream, pale, hair gold as broomflower, eyes green as leaves and heart of oak. I felt now the sun on my skin as once I had taken its sweetness into my leaves. The light bit into my eyes.

Lleu fell in love with the woman who rose fully formed from the land, fashioned by magic to be perfect for him in every way. Every way.

In his way he loved me but I loved the scent of the soil, the feel of rain on my flesh, on my tongue, the touch of the wind.

He took me to a castle, with walls of stone, uprooted from the earth like me, shaped, like me, into a new unnatural form. Like me. I was given as a gift to this man as some would give a bunch of flowers.

People said when I entered a room a honeysweet scent would fill the air.

I missed the taste of earth, sweet minerals, feeding on sunshine, the kiss of moonlight.

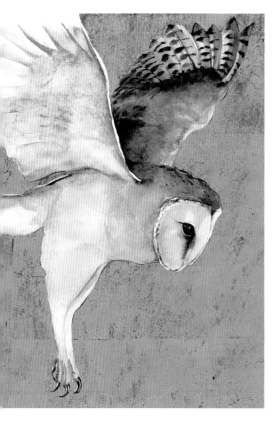

I missed the many moths and bees, butterflies and insects who had brushed my stamen, pollinated my flowers, fed from the nectar.

I tried to understand the ways of men.

But human ways of love seemed harsh.

I missed the voices of the plants, the song of the earth that would thrill my roots.

Lleu would not take me with him when he hunted.

And so it was that one day when he was gone and I, alone in the stone walls dreamed of the touch of bees; another rode by.

The stag he chased was almost spent.

Lonely.

I sent a servant out to discover who this was, who hunted so close to our castle. I asked if he would come in, rest, eat.

It was only when I saw this man that I understood what Lleu meant when he said he loved me. I gave my heart to Gronw Pebr. He saw the wildness trapped inside my green eyes. His touch made my human self whole for the first time. Wild and human united in my form and I gloried in being made flesh.

For though I had been conjured to be the perfect wife for Lleu, he was not made for me. All night I learned the ways of love, and now I no longer desired the touch of bees and blessed the day Math took me from the mountain's side.

The desire to love was so strong, I killed my husband to be with Gronw.

If Math thought, when he ripped away my human form and made me owl, that he had punished me, then he was wrong. I have been changed so many times, been so many things, seed, to plant, to flower and tree to flesh and bone.

Now I hunt the twilight times, the blue hour, on hushed wings, breast white as meadowsweet, pale gold back like broom, claws like thorns and heart of oak, wedded to the air, to the night.

Flight gives me freedom.

And I would always rather be owl than flowers, for now I can still hear the wild song of the night, I have wings for flight, and I have eyes to look upon the beauty of wild things.

The Owl in Art
and Literature

Aristophanes

The Greek playwright Aristophanes, in his play *The Birds*, dating from 414 BC, says of 'owls', (the nickname of the owl-embossed silver coin the tetradrachm) as being the best as 'they will dwell in your home and nest in your purse, hatching out small change'.

Aesop's Fables

Naturally, in the sixth century BC, Aesop has a fable about the owl. The owl offers the other birds pearls of wisdom concerning the destroying of: trees that will harbour mistletoe which will be used to kill birds, flax that will be used to make nets to catch birds, and archers who will fletch their arrows with feathers and then kill birds. The other birds laugh at the owl and think it mad. However, in time all the predictions come true, by which time it is too late for them to make amends and the owl no longer offers up any suggestions to them but sits in silence.

The Fables of Bidpai

The *Panchatantra*, known in English as *The Fables of Bidpai* is an Indian text believed to be from the third century BC. It contains many animal fables in prose and verse and was originally, as are many early collected texts, almost certainly from an oral tradition. There are known to be over two hundred versions in over fifty languages and has it has been expanded, contracted and reworked along the way. Not surprisingly perhaps this collection has several owl stories and one is rather horrific.

The story *Kākolūkīyam, Of Crows and Owls*, starts from the premise that the owl and the crow are sworn enemies. One of the crows, pretending he is no longer allowed into his own crow 'gang', works his way into the owl group to find out their secrets. Having gained all the knowledge he can, he calls up his crow cronies and they block the entrances to the owl cave, where they start a fire. All the owls are suffocated and perish.

Pliny the Elder

Pliny the Elder in his *Natural History* of 77 AD has a more authentic explanation of how the owl was viewed. 'If he be seen to fly either within cities, or otherwise abroad in any place, it is not for good, but prognosticates some fearful misfortune'.

Bestiary

(with extracts from *Giraldus Cambrensis* on Irish birds. England, possibly from Salisbury)

Written in Latin in the second quarter of the thirteenth century, this *Bestiary* is part of The Harley Collection held by the British Library. Originally collected by Robert (1661–1724) and Edward (1689–1741) Harley, 1st and 2nd earls of Oxford and Mortimer, the manuscript was sold to the nation in 1753 by the widow and daughter of the latter and form one of the foundation collections of the British Library.

Bestiaries were originally considered to be purely natural history books, written on parchment with very detailed and highly decorated initial letters in varying depths; this owl (right) is very large, at eleven lines deep. It would seem from more recent research however, that the high moral tone of bestiary manuscripts meant they were often used as inspiration for sermons. The equation of owls with Jews will be discussed in the next section but it is perhaps worth mentioning here that the owl was seen as the outsider, the lone wanderer in darkness. They were often attacked by other birds if seen during daylight hours, particularly corvids as witnessed by the obvious magpie in this illustration.

sumus quelibet peccorem. Bubo

The Owl and The Nightingale

The Middle English poem from the twelfth or thirteenth century AD, *The Owl and The Nightingale* is a famous text with no confirmed date of composition, author or origin; in spite of the fact that there are two original manuscripts surviving. It is by way of a conversation poem, reported by an unspecified narrator, with the nightingale generally being rude and the owl rebuffing her. Here are the main threads in their simplest form.

Nightingale: 'Owl you are ugly and unclean.'

Owl: 'I suggest we should be civil to each other.'

Nightingale: 'You make horrid shrieks and screeches and your night-time activity is based on vice and hatred.'

Owl: 'You make a lot of noise and you are boring.'

Nightingale: 'Your song is gloomy.'

Owl: 'You only sing in summer, which makes men feel lustful; it's your only talent and I serve the church by ridding them of rats.'

Nightingale: 'My songs inspire the congregation to think of heaven and make them more pious.'

Owl: 'My song helps the people repent their decisions in life and your flowery bright tunes can lead women to promiscuous relations.'

Nightingale: 'You are no use except when dead as a scarecrow used by farmers.'

Owl: 'I agree, I can even help man after death.'

Things start to escalate as each side proposes getting their friends (songbirds and raptors) to side with them. A sensible wren intervenes and suggests asking Nicholas of Guildford to make a judgement. The poem ends with the two protagonists flying off to find Nicholas who lived at Portesham in Dorset.

Tickling owls

In an unpublished lecture, Rabbi Dr. Charles Middleburgh, Dean of Leo Baeck College, London, discussed the text of the medieval bestiary MS Bodley 764 housed in Oxford's Bodleian Library which says:

This bird signifies the Jews who when our Lord came to save them rejected him, saying 'We have no king except Caesar', and preferred the darkness to the light. (The Old Testament views the owl as unclean and living in solitary desolation.)

'This analogy, it seems to me, is flattering to neither Jews nor Owls and is more reflective of the opinions of the thirteenth-century author than those he denigrates.

'That the designation of Jews as creatures of the dark, like owls, might have been more widespread than perhaps imagined in the medieval world may be demonstrated by an illumination

in the famous *Brother Haggadah*, dated to the fourteenth century and demonstrating a mix of stylistic elements. On one page, associated with the Bitter Herbs eaten at the Passover seder meal, there is an illumination which depicts the torso of a bearded, probably Jewish, figure whose pointing finger is among the feathers of a downy, black owl chick.

'It is worth conjecturing that the smiling Jew is not actually just pointing to the owl but tickling it, a gentle in-house mockery of medieval Christianity's equation of Jews with owls, subverting an otherwise bitter analogy.'

Misericords

Misericords are the carved shelf on the top edge of a drop-down seat in a church and were usually used to give respite to those standing for long prayers. In medieval churches these little gems, hidden in the choir stalls, often told stories of church and state or nature as well. Sometimes they were created as a tiny subversive 'joke' between the carver and the user. There are many depictions of owls amongst misericords (above, from Norwich Cathedral) we see the owl being mobbed by massed birds. Also from Norwich, what I interpret to be a bird conference with the owl holding forth with gesturing wing. This image (above right) is particularly good for showing how the underside of the seat was often laid out with secondary carvings in the bottom corners.

However, I would suggest that the image from Ely cathedral (right) was done by someone who really admired the bird. The lovely detail of the head and the claw holding the mouse speak of an artist who loved and knew his subject.

La Fontaine

Moving on to seventeenth century France, we find Jean de La Fontaine, whose fabled *Fables* are considered great literary masterpieces, has one about *The Eagle and the Owl*. In elegant rhyming couplets he explains how the two birds, previously sworn enemies, decide to make a pact whereby they don't predate each other's offspring; but how to tell if it IS the offspring of their friend? The owl says this will be easy as his chicks are so very beautiful, the eagle will recognize them at once: 'Well formed and fine, with pretty sparkling eyes; Nothing around to equal them you'll find.' We can surmise what will happen and so it comes to pass. The eagle one day finds a nest with the owl's chicks and thinks them 'Grim little monsters, fitted but to shock' and so he eats them. The moral of course, is that children always look beautiful to their parents!

John Gay

In 1727, the playwright John Gay, best known for *The Beggar's Opera*, wrote *Fifty-one Fables in Verse* and naturally there is one about an owl, well two owls actually.

A sparrow overhears two owls discussing, 'How is the modern taste decayed! Where's the respect to wisdom paid?' The sparrow suggests that, instead of bemoaning lost glories, they should get on with the job of catching mice and then everyone would love them again.

Shakespeare and Sir Walter Scott

Shakespeare mentioned the owl hoot preceding a death in both Macbeth and Julius Caesar, and 'the bird of doom' was well known as Sir Walter Scott writing in 1819 said:
Birds of omen dark and foul,
Night-crow, raven, bat, and owl,
Leave the sick man to his dream–
All night long he heard your scream.

William Wordsworth

The poet William Wordsworth wrote about an owl in his autobiographical poem 'The Prelude'. This extract comes from the earliest manuscript of 1799, MS JJ. (There were two other versions but none of them were published during his lifetime.)

In this version he writes as though he were the boy calling the owls; in later versions, the scene is described in the third person.

There was a boy ye knew him well, ye rocks
And islands of Winander & ye green
Peninsulas of Esthwaite many a time
When the stars began
To move along the edges of the hills
Rising or setting would he stand alone
Beneath the trees or by the glimmering lakes
And through his fingers woven in one close knot
Blow mimic hootings to the silent owls
And bid them answer him.
And they would shout
Across the wat'ry vale & shout again
Responsive to my call with tremulous sobs
And long halloos & screams & echoes loud
Redoubled & redoubled a wild scene
Of mirth & jocund din.

Florence Nightingale

One very famous owl keeper was Florence Nightingale. Rescued in 1850 in Athens and hand reared, her pet owl Athena, a little owl, was carried in her pocket and showed exemplary loyalty to her mistress, using her very sharp beak to keep back anyone she thought was coming too close. Florence had the bird for five years and she was a great favourite. Due to work in the Crimea, she was getting ready to go and left Athena in the care of relatives. In the hurry and confusion they left the owl alone in the attic and, too domesticated to hunt and shocked by loneliness, she was found dead when they finally checked on her. Florence had not left yet and so, devastated by the loss, she had her darling embalmed and stuffed, in which state the owl stayed with her until her death in 1910. On holding the dead Athena and weeping, she said, 'Poor little beastie, it was odd how much I loved you.' Her sister Parthenope, Lady Verney, catalogued Florence's life with the bird in her book *The Life and Death of Athena an Owlet from the Parthenon*, with handwritten text and drawings. Parthenope had just a few copies self-published and sent one out to cheer her sister who was ill in the Crimea.

Edward Lear

Edward Lear is probably best known today for his nonsense verse but from an early age he actually earned his money as an illustrator. He could also be called a musician and composer too because he wrote many settings of the poetry of Tennyson as well as songs for his own works like *The Owl and the Pussycat*. This most famous of his poems was first published in *Nonsense Songs, Stories, Botany and Alphabets* in 1871 and was originally written for the children of his patron Edward Stanley, 13th Earl of Derby. Lear loved the flexibility of the English language; witness his 'Quangle-Wangle' and the 'Pobble' to name but two. Possibly his most famous word invention is 'runcible' in *The Owl and the Pussycat*, a nonsense word now to be found in most dictionaries.

The Owl and the Pussycat

The Owl and the Pussycat went to sea
In a beautiful pea-green boat,
They took some honey, and plenty of money,
Wrapped up in a five pound note.
The Owl looked up to the stars above,
And sang to a small guitar,
"O lovely Pussy! O Pussy, my love,
What a beautiful Pussy you are, you are, you are,
What a beautiful Pussy you are."

Pussy said to the Owl, "You elegant fowl,
How charmingly sweet you sing.
O let us be married, too long we have tarried;
But what shall we do for a ring?"
They sailed away, for a year and a day,
To the land where the Bong-tree grows,
And there in a wood a Piggy-wig stood
With a ring at the end of his nose, his nose, his nose,
With a ring at the end of his nose.

"Dear Pig, are you willing to sell for one shilling
your ring?" Said the Piggy, "I will"
So they took it away, and were married next day
By the Turkey who lives on the hill.
They dined on mince, and slices of quince,
Which they ate with a runcible spoon.
And hand in hand, on the edge of the sand,
They danced by the light of the moon, the moon, the moon,
They danced by the light of the moon.

The Tale of Squirrel Nutkin
by Beatrix Potter

Perhaps surprisingly, an owl called Old Brown features centre stage in Beatrix Potter's 1903 book, *The Tale of Squirrel Nutkin*. Old Brown lives on an island in the middle of a lake. Potter stayed at Lingholm in the Lake District in 1901 where she started drawing and writing Nutkin, and Derwentwater and St. Hubert's Island can clearly be seen in her illustrations as the models for the lake and the island.

Nutkin and his squirrel chums bring the owl offerings to secure the rights to collecting nuts on his island and they cross the water every day with their little nut sacks and cross back in the evening. (Regarding the offerings, interestingly, although we see a picture of the squirrels fishing and the idea of them collecting beetles seems possible, there is never any explanation of how they catch the mice and the mole that are two of the earlier owl gifts in the story!)

This is the tale of a tail and it has parallels with fairy tales in many cultures. The threatening figure living alone and ready to reap vengeance on the 'innocents' is all too familiar. On each of the six consecutive days the squirrels visit the island, they bring Old Brown a gift and each day the naughty Nutkin goads the owl with a riddle. (Riddles were popular at the time and here, the riddles are left for the reader to interpret.) The owl, however, does not respond and gradually the squirrel gets braver and braver, until finally he jumps on the owl's head;

'Then all at once there was a flutterment and a scufflement and a loud "Squeak!"'

The other squirrels scuttered away into the bushes.

When they came back very cautiously, peeping round the tree—there was Old Brown sitting on his door-step, quite still, with his eyes closed, as if nothing had happened. But Nutkin was in his waistcoat pocket!'

When Nutkin reappears to join his friends, having been taken inside Old Brown's house, we see that the owl has got his own back by removing half of Nutkin's tail.

It is an exposition about the link between actions and consequences.

Wol from *Winnie-the-Pooh*

Wol was not a stuffed toy belonging to Christopher Robin Milne as the other animals were, so when E.H. Shepard drew the illustrations of the inhabitants of the Hundred Acre Wood, he drew him as a real bird. All the other animals who populate A.A. Milne's famous books about Winnie the Pooh think Wol is very clever, the truth being, however, that he is not. His grasp of reading and writing is somewhat sketchy, witnessed by the way he spells his name, and many anxious moments ensue through the stories as people ask him to pass judgement on things he can't really read.

Wol has a whiff of the owl in the fables we have met already in the myths and legends chapter of this book, always slightly overreaching himself.

James Thurber

James Thurber (1894-1961) was a very famous American cartoonist, writer, humourist and journalist; probably best known in the UK today for *The Life of Walter Mitty,* a short story of his later adapted into a film twice, in 1947 and 2013. Thurber himself disliked the one made in his lifetime. He wrote over seventy-five short fables, many of which were first published in The New Yorker and subsequently collected into *Fables for Our Time and Famous Poems Illustrated* (1940) and *Further Fables for Our Time* (1956). These tales are all rather unexpected and have a sharp, pithy, one line moral. In, for instance, *The Little Girl and the Wolf*, a reworking of the *Little Red Riding Hood* story, the final line is 'So the little girl took an automatic out of her basket and shot the wolf dead.' (Moral: It is not so easy to fool little girls nowadays as it used to be.)

Thurber wrote a famous story about an owl, which has the bird, as we have seen before, thinking himself above the other birds and animals and afraid to admit his defects.

Thurber wrote a famous story about an owl which has the bird, as we have seen before, thinking himself above the other birds and animals and afraid to admit his defects. In *The Owl who was God* we meet an owl who, through a series of wonderfully, if completely unintentionally, well-timed responses to questions is believed by the other animals to be the fount of all knowledge and wisdom. Not only can he see perfectly in the dark, he is seemingly able to tackle issues of language and philosophy without having to pause for thought:

Secretary Bird: 'Can you give me another expression for 'that is to say' or 'namely'?'

Owl: 'To wit.'

Secretary Bird: 'Why does the lover call on his love?'

Owl: 'To woo.'

The admiration of the other animals is secured, in spite of reservations voiced by some about his ability to see in daylight, and he is approached about becoming leader. He agrees and with slow steps and staring eyes he comes before them at noon; appearing to the assembled creatures as dignified and important rather than simply short-sighted. 'He is God' they exclaim, and begin to follow him everywhere; even along the concrete road and under the wheels of an oncoming truck which he, of course, has failed to see or even acknowledge when it's pointed out to him (on hearing of the oncoming truck Secretary Bird asks 'aren't you afraid?' to which the owl simply replies 'Who?')

Most of the animals are killed, including the owl, and Thurber's moral is established - you can fool too many of the people too much of the time.

www.frankduffy.co.uk

Pablo Picasso

Through his life Picasso produced a series of wonderful owl vases and he seemed to have a particular connection to the bird.

Françoise Gilot, Picasso's partner, wrote in her autobiography, *Life with Picasso*, how, as a regular keeper of birds, he did at one time have an owl. Initially the relationship was rather taxing for both parties, with the owl screeching at Picasso and he swearing obscenities back. The owl consistently bit Picasso's finger but, owing to the skin on his hands being very tough, he persevered and eventually the owl would let itself be scratched on the head and perch on his finger rather than biting it. According to Gilot, however, it never really looked happy.

The Owl Service
by Alan Garner

No chapter looking at owls in literature should fail to mention one of the most influential 'owl' stories of the 1960s, Alan Garner's seminal work *The Owl Service*, a chilling reworking of the story of Bloduwedd (re-told previously in this book by Jackie Morris). Garner has the love triangle enacted by teenagers in a quiet Welsh valley, with the help of an owl-decorated dinner service.

The dinner service in question was owned by Alan Garner's future parents-in-law and he first saw it when having dinner with them. He had been thinking about the Bloduwedd legend and it was instrumental in the writing of *The Owl Service*. The plates, when seen from the rim, look like they have a pattern of flowers but when seen from the middle the design looks like an owl. Although the story is marketed as a children's book, the themes, attitudes and foreboding creepiness place it firmly within the list of those books written for children but which are read by adults as well. If you have never read it do, you will not be disappointed. Garner won the prestigious Carnegie Medal for this book in the same year that he won the Guardian Children's Fiction Prize; only five other books have won both. Garner has written many other books of great distinction but *The Owl Service* remains perhaps one of his best known novels to date.

Note on the plate design. The original design is by Christopher Dresser, who was very famous in his lifetime and has been referred to as the 'Father of Industrial Design'. During the late 1800s he worked for major ceramic manufacturers including Minton and Wedgwood. Dresser worked not only in ceramics but metal, furniture, glass and textiles and a major collection of his work can be found at the Dorman Museum in Middlesbrough, including an example of the plate, which was donated to the museum in 2017 by Griselda and Alan Garner, to commemorate the fiftieth anniversary of the publication of *The Owl Service*. Another plate is in Alan Garner's archive at the Bodleian Library.

Harry Potter

Finally, as Harry Potter is a literary beacon for hundreds and thousands of children from 1997 to the present, one has to mention that his owl Hedwig is a snowy owl, played in the films by one called Gizmo with Ook and Sprout as his main stand-ins. Hedwig was a real character in the books, who offered companionship and solace to Harry, particularly when he lived with the muggle (non-wizard) Dursley family after the death of his parents.

Ashridge

Below Butland Wood I stop to watch
the barn owl beat its slow silence, valley long,
ghost white against the beeches.

Dropping now to the farm tucked up in dusk
I hear those small unnoticed sounds return;
the hill's herd, the sea beyond,
slow breath, that pulse in my ear.

Dru Marland

From *Drawn Chorus – an alphabet of birds*
(Gert Macky Books, 2017)

Timorous

The field mouse lives a precarious life
poised on a razor's edge.
Skittering through the grass at night,
her ears attuned to
stealthy stoats,
wicked weasels
furtive foxes
and
bumbling badgers --
she misses
the owl
whose dagger claws
seize her from above
and break her back.

Charles Middleburgh

Gather round, I will tell you a story

Owl Power

They say in the local sanctuary
owls are the stupidest creatures
all this wisdom business is
the mythological media at work
but the shortest nosing into books
tells you even the mythic world
is bamboozled by the creature – no
two cultures being able to agree

The bird was cherished by Minerva
hebrews loathed it as unclean
buddhists treasure its seclusion
elsewhere night-hag evil omen

The baker's daughter's silly cry
ungrateful chinese children
the precious life of Genghis Khan
sweet fodder to the owl's blink

In the end it's the paradox
I'll be what you want romantic fool
that scares elates about the owl
sitting in the dark and seeing all

not true, not true the cynics say
the bloody fraudster's almost blind
dead lazy till its stomach rattles
its skill is seeing with its ears

Ruthlessness stupidity
(transmogrified to wisdom)
make the perfect pitch for power
so proofed – why give a hoot for gods

Rg Gregory

Sedgemoor

The final lunge of sunlight
in evening's falling green. A barn owl
hunts the serried hedgerows, the marching trees.

Skirl of white and skirmish. Night cries are cut short
by its heart-stopping
drop, the eternal mercy of drawn steel.

Sacrificial gifts of blood
for ghosts who moulder in this earth,
their murder fields.

Deborah Harvey

No Malice Shown

See the owl in swift silent flight,
Surfing the darkness of the night,
In control of its black domain,
Its prey killed quick, no time for pain.

Don't be outraged when it's victim dies;
The owl's not a mugger of the skies,
No malice shown when it hunts for meat,
It leaves alone what it cannot eat!

Clive Blake

From *View Points and Points of View* by Clive Blake (poetry)
and Chris Robbins (photography).

Little Lieutenant

The best of owls come in small packages.
Unaware of his comparative lack of stature,
This is no wise, imposing or regal bird.

Rather, he seems a serious, busy sort of fellow,
Wearing his bright and beady yellow eyes
Like insignia to indicate his credentials.

He has places to be, and no time for time-wasters
You don't want to meet with his disapproving brow.

His plump, jaunty body may cause you to smirk
But with a head-down, bearing-down, extended trot
This little lieutenant is not one to be scoffed at.

Meredith Russ

Owl Cabins
Bordeaux, south west France

The artist/architect collective Bruit de Frigo have been running a *Les Refuges Periurbains* campaign (translates as 'peri-urban shelters'). They have identified the zone between city and countryside which is often neglected these urban fringes, in spite of a general feeling that they can't possibly have anything to offer, are actually nature within touching distance of the city. Bruit de Frigo thinks that they should be reevaluated as an urban resource.

They have a three step approach to getting people into these spaces. Firstly actually confirming where these places are and what they could be used for (walking, cycling, running, camping). Secondly, they have designed and built artwork shelters within each designated area and finally, setting out how each cabin can be used.

Around the city of Bordeaux an urban green hike has been created, with a target of five to six days to cover the whole loop. A total of ten shelters (rather like the huts found in the mountains for anyone to use – no electricity, no water, just a safe sleeping space) are being created to give walkers an unforgettable rest experience in nature.

These part sculpture, part architecture cabins, are stunning to look at and exciting to sleep in. The ones of particular interest here are the three *Les Guetteurs* or The Watchers. Three back to back owls sitting companionably on the banks of the local wetlands provide a sleeping refuge for six people in three pairs. Made from treated plywood, the cabins have three floors, circular white beds and a boardwalk overlooking the water.

All the cabins are free to use. To look at the other amazing designs created so far go to www.zebra3.org/les-refuges-periurbains. The cabins are well used during the hiking season, not necessarily for sleep-overs but as a focal point for family get togethers or picnics and once or twice a year the Bordeaux Métropole organises a two-day collective suburban hike with up to eighty participants.

Les Refuges Periurbains is financed by Bordeaux Métropole, initiated by Bruit du Frigo, (a creative collective looking at urban living) and the cabins were made by Zebra3, who used different artists and designers to create constructions outside the usual realm of what is possible.

Photo credits and artworks by chapter

page 104: Kevin Sawford
page 105: National Film Board of Canada
pages 106: Lennart Larsen, National Museum, Denmark
page 107: Trevor Clifford
pages 108 &109: Jane Russ
pages 110–114: **Blodeuwedd by Jackie Morris www.jackiemorris.co.uk**

The Owl in Art and Literature
page 116: **'Owl King' by Hannah Willow pastel and gold leaf. www.facebook.com/ Hannah.willow.artist**
page 118 top: Illustration of Aesop's fable 'The Owl and Other Birds'
page 118 btm: Dimitri's Kamaras – Numismatic Museum of Athens
page 119: Kalîla and Dimma of Bidpai, Syriac painter, c. 1310
page 121: British Library
page 123: British Library
page 124 & 125 top: Norwich Cathedral by Eric Webb
page 125 btm: Ely Cathedral by Eric Webb
page 127: **Owl in Flight on chain by Hairy Growler. www.hairygrowler.com**
page 129: Florence Nightingale standing with owl, Wellcome Library
page 130: **'The Owl and The Pussycat', stained glass panel by Tamsin Abbott. www.tamsinabbott.co.uk**
page 131 & 132: Edward Lear
page 133: **'In a Beautiful Pea-Green Boat' by Eleanor Bartleman. www.eleanorbartleman.co.uk**
page 134, 135 & 136: Beatrix Potter
page 137: **'Tu-whit Tu-Who, a merry note', linocut by Celia Hart. www.celiahart.co.uk**
page 138: Original Winnie-the-Pooh stuffed toys on display at the Stephen
A. Schwarzman Building, New York.
page 141: **'Owl' by Frank Duffy www.frankduffy.co.uk**
page 142: JD Falk
page 143: **'Edyth – Barn Owl' by Kate Wyatt www.katewyattartist.co.uk kathwyatt@btinternet.com**
page 144: Drawn realisation of the owl service plate by Jane Russ
page 147: Catriona Komlosi
page 146 & 147: **Leather work and hand coloured owl bag and side panel by Skyravenwolf/photography by Dru Marland**
page 148: **'Night Owl', pyrographic carving by Jen Heart at Of Half Imagined Things.** This bone (probably from a cow) was found by Jen and the design worked directly onto it.
ofhalfimaginedthings.bigcartel.com
page 149: **Hollow-bodied copper weathervane. www.greensvanes.co.uk**
page 150: **'The Storyteller' by Jenny Steer. Illustration and wood burnings on birchwood. www.jennysteer.com**
page 153: **'Owls Not Flowers' by Catherine Hyde. www.catherinehyde.co.uk**
page 154: Pot by Margaret Brampton
page 157: **'The Watchers', designed and built by Zébra3 Bordeaux**

Endpapers: **Jane Russ**

Acknowledgements

The hugest, biggest possible thank you to the wonderful photographers and artists who have stepped up to the plate yet again. I could not do it without you and I am so thrilled that you trust me with your images.

The wonderful Jackie Morris continues to most generously produce a story for me and allow me to use one of her images.

Many thanks to my chum and sister-in-heart Gilly Middleburgh; your proofing continues to be my long-stop of excellence.

Matthew Howard at Graffeg for continuing to believe I could do this thing.

And finally, for his continued support with every book, I would like to acknowledge and thank my long-suffering husband Mick Toole.

The Owl Book
Published in Great Britain in 2018 by Graffeg Limited

Written by Jane Russ copyright © 2018. Designed and produced by Graffeg Limited copyright © 2018

This edition published 2020.

Graffeg Limited, 24 Stradey Park Business Centre, Mwrwg Road, Llangennech, Llanelli, Carmarthenshire SA14 8YP Wales UK Tel 01554 824000 www.graffeg.com

Jane Russ is hereby identified as the author of this work in accordance with section 77 of the Copyrights, Designs and Patents Act 1988.

A CIP Catalogue record for this book is available from the British Library.

ISBN 9781912050420

2 3 4 5 6 7 8 9